I0416595

SAVING TOO

CAN

MAKE YOU RICH

David Mark

i

Copyright © 2024 David Mark

All rights reserved.

ISBN:

DEDICATION

To those who believe in the transformative power of a single dollar saved, and to the dreamers who envision wealth not as an unattainable mirage but as a tangible reality woven from the fabric of disciplined financial choices. This book is dedicated to the seekers of prosperity who understand that the journey to riches begins with a humble step towards saving.

To the prudent spirits and to the common heroes who have used diligence and foresight to turn small savings into a solid foundation for their aspirations. Your tales provide inspiration for the story told in these pages and offer hope to anyone who dares to think they can be wealthy.

To the mentors, whose wisdom has illuminated the way, this dedication is a tribute to your collective wisdom, a timeless gift that continues to shape the financial destinies of those willing to listen and learn.

To the strong-willed individuals who have survived financial hardships and come out stronger because they understand that saving money is a means that promotes security, independence, and endless future. May this book be a companion, guiding navigating the seas of financial uncertainty. With them toward the shores of lasting gratitude and admiration for those dedicated potential of every saved penny, t'

DEDICATION

To those who believe in the transformative power of a single dollar saved, and to the dreamers who envision wealth not as an unattainable mirage but as a tangible reality woven from the fabric of disciplined financial choices. This book is dedicated to the seekers of prosperity who understand that the journey to riches begins with a humble step towards saving.

To the prudent spirits and to the common heroes who have used diligence and foresight to turn small savings into a solid foundation for their aspirations. Your tales provide inspiration for the story told in these pages and offer hope to anyone who dares to think they can be wealthy.

To the mentors, whose wisdom has illuminated the way, this dedication is a tribute to your collective wisdom, a timeless gift that continues to shape the financial destinies of those willing to listen and learn.

To the strong-willed individuals who have survived financial hardships and come out stronger because they understand that saving money is a mentality that promotes security, independence, and an endless future. May this book be a compass for those navigating the seas of financial uncertainty, guiding them toward the shores of lasting prosperity. With gratitude and admiration for the believers in the potential of every saved penny, this work is dedicated to you – for understanding that **"Saving Too Can Make You Rich."**

ACKNOWLEDGEMENT

This book is the result of collective effort and support, and I am deeply grateful to those who have contributed to its creation. My heartfelt thanks to my family for their unwavering support, friends and colleagues for their valuable insights, mentors for sharing their wisdom, and early reviewers for their feedback.

Special appreciation goes to the publishing team whose dedication turned words into reality. To the readers, your engagement has been inspiring. Finally, a heartfelt thank you to the individuals whose stories of financial resilience form the heart of this book – your journeys are the driving force behind these pages.

This work is a collaboration, and I extend my sincere thanks to everyone involved for helping bring **"Saving Too Can Make You Rich"** to life.

Table of Contents

INTRODUCTION 1

THE POWER OF SAVING 5

SETTING THE STAGE FOR FINANCIAL SUCCESS 7

THE PSYCHOLOGY OF MONEY 9

CHAPTER 1 11

THE FOUNDATION OF WEALTH 11

Understanding the Importance of Saving 12

Building a Solid Financial Foundation 14

Breaking Free from the Cycle of Living from Paycheck to Paycheck 16

CHAPTER 2 19

BUDGETING BASICS 19

The Art of Budgeting.. 20

Creating a Realistic Spending Plan 23

Identify & Eliminate Financial Risks 25

CHAPTER 3 27

THE MAGIC OF COMPOUND INTEREST 27

Unveiling the Eighth Wonder of the World 28

Harnessing the Power of Time in Investing 32

Maximizing Returns through Compound Growth............ 35

CHAPTER 4 37

OVERCOMING SAVING MYTH & OBSTACLES 37

Dispelling Common Misconceptions 38

Navigating Emotional Challenges in Savings.................... 40

Strategies for Consistent and Sustainable savings 43

CHAPTER 5 45

   THE MINDSET OF FINANCIAL SUCCESS 45

      Cultivating a Wealth-Building Mindset 45

      Aligning Financial Goals with Personal Values................. 48

      Fostering a Healthy Relationship with Money................. 50

CHAPTER 6 53

   REAL LIFE STORIES OF FINANCIAL TRANSFORMATION 53

      Real Life Stories of Financial Transformation................... 53

      Learning from the Journeys of Financial Success 56

      Turning Adversity into Financial Triumph 59

CHAPTER 7 61

   INVESTING IN YOUR FUTURE 61

      Beyond Saving: The Role of Investing 61

      Diversifying Your Investment Portfolio 62

      Balancing Risk and Reward 64

CHAPTER 8 67

   NAVIGATING ECONOMIC UNCERTAINTY 67

      Building Resilience in Financial Planning 67

      Strategies for Thriving in Turbulent Times........................ 68

      Adapting to Changing Financial Landscapes.................... 71

   Conclusion.. 74

   About the Author.. 76

INTRODUCTION

In the symphony of financial wisdom, the voices of history's most influential figures resonate with timeless lessons on the art of saving. Let us draw inspiration from the words of not just one luminary but several, as we weave a tapestry of insights that enrich our understanding of the transformative power of saving.

Warren Buffett, the Oracle of Omaha and one of the most successful investors of our time, imparts a nugget of financial sagacity: *"Do not save what is left after spending, but spend what is left after saving."* This mantra encapsulates the essence of disciplined financial management, urging us to prioritize saving before succumbing to the allure of discretionary spending. Buffett's philosophy emphasizes that wealth is not determined by what we earn but rather by what we choose to save and invest wisely.

As we traverse the corridors of financial history, **John D. Rockefeller**, the American business magnate and philanthropist, adds his voice to the conversation: *"The secret to success is to know something nobody else knows."* In the realm of personal finance, this insight speaks to the importance of acquiring financial knowledge and making informed decisions. By understanding the principles of saving, investing, and wealth preservation, we gain a distinct advantage on our journey toward financial prosperity.

The eminent **Maya Angelou**, renowned for her poetic wisdom, offers a perspective that transcends the monetary realm: "We can learn to see each other and see ourselves in each other and recognize that human beings are more alike than we are unalike." In the context of saving, Angelou's words remind us that financial success is not just an individual endeavor; it is a shared experience that can uplift communities and foster collective well-being. The act of saving, when approached conscientiously, extends beyond personal enrichment to become a force for positive change on a broader scale.

Now, let's revisit the world of economics through the lens of **Albert Einstein**, whose brilliance extends beyond theoretical physics: *"Compound interest is the eighth wonder of the world. He who understands it, earns it; he who doesn't, pays it."* Einstein's perspective on compound interest illuminates the compounding magic that unfolds when we diligently save and invest over time. By harnessing the power of compound growth, we create a financial trajectory that propels us toward prosperity.

In this rich tapestry of quotes, we find a chorus of voices echoing the sentiment that saving is not merely a financial strategy but a mindset, a way of life that extends its influence into every aspect of our existence.

As we navigate the chapters ahead, let Franklin's words serve as a beacon, inspiring us to adopt a discerning perspective on our financial choices. Together, let us delve deeper into the world of saving, armed with the wisdom of those who have tread this path before us, and discover how the accumulation of small savings can indeed make us rich in ways that extend beyond our financial portfolios.

THE POWER OF SAVING

The power of saving extends far beyond the mere accumulation of money in a bank account; it is a transformative force that shapes the course of one's financial destiny. Saving is not merely a financial activity; it is a mindset, a deliberate choice to allocate resources thoughtfully with an eye on the future. Let's explore the profound implications of this seemingly simple act.

At its core, saving empowers individuals to take control of their financial narratives. It is the foundation upon which dreams are built, providing a sense of security and freedom. When we save, we create a safety net that shields us from unforeseen circumstances and unexpected expenses, offering peace of mind in the face of life's uncertainties.

Moreover, the power of saving lies in its compounding effect. Every dollar set aside has the potential to grow over time, thanks to the magic of compound interest. This exponential growth transforms small, consistent contributions into a substantial financial foundation. By allowing money to work for us, we unlock the door to financial prosperity and open up opportunities that might have seemed out of reach.

Saving is also a powerful tool for achieving long-term goals. Whether it's buying a home, funding education, or retiring comfortably, disciplined saving provides the means to turn aspirations into reality. It empowers individuals to navigate life's milestones with confidence, knowing that they have cultivated the financial resources to support their dreams.

Beyond the numerical aspect, saving cultivates a mindset of discipline and delayed gratification. It encourages individuals to distinguish between needs and wants, fostering a conscious and intentional approach to spending. In doing so, it lays the groundwork for responsible financial behavior, a skill that transcends the realm of personal finance and extends into various aspects of life.

Furthermore, the power of saving is egalitarian; it is accessible to anyone willing to embrace it. Regardless of income level or financial expertise, the act of saving is a universal principle that can be adopted by individuals from all walks of life. It democratizes the journey to financial well-being, making wealth accumulation a possibility for those who are committed to making incremental steps toward their goals.

In essence, saving is not just about accumulating money; it is a dynamic force that empowers individuals to shape their financial destinies. It is a journey that transcends the mere preservation of dollars and cents, evolving into a path of financial literacy, resilience, and ultimately, lasting prosperity. Embracing the power of saving is an investment in oneself—an investment that pays dividends not only in financial terms but also in the peace of mind, freedom, and opportunities it affords along the way.

SETTING THE STAGE FOR FINANCIAL SUCCESS

Setting the stage for financial success involves laying a solid foundation built on principles of discipline, strategic planning, and a clear vision for the future. This process not only requires understanding the mechanics of personal finance but also adopting a mindset that positions financial goals as achievable milestones. As we embark on this journey, let us draw inspiration from the testimony of a global business magnate whose success story exemplifies the essence of setting the stage for financial triumph.

One of the most iconic entrepreneurs of our time, Richard Branson, the founder of the Virgin Group, offers a testimony that resonates with the principles of financial success. Branson's journey is a testament to the transformative power of strategic decision-making, resilience, and the ability to envision and pursue ambitious goals. His venture into the music industry, airlines, telecommunications, and various other sectors demonstrates a keen understanding of diversification and calculated risk-taking.

Branson's success story underscores the importance of setting the stage for financial success by embracing a mindset of innovation and adaptability. His ability to identify opportunities, take calculated risks, and remain resilient in the face of challenges has been pivotal to his financial ascent. It reflects the essence of laying a foundation that is not only strong but also flexible, capable of weathering the inevitable storms that come with the pursuit of success.

On a more personal level, setting the stage for financial success involves creating a roadmap that aligns with one's aspirations. It means setting clear financial goals, whether it be homeownership, education, retirement, or entrepreneurial endeavors, and devising a strategic plan to achieve them. This could include crafting a budget, managing debt wisely, and investing judiciously, all while maintaining a disciplined approach to saving.

The testimony of Richard Branson serves as a source of inspiration, illustrating that the journey to financial success is not a linear path but a dynamic process marked by adaptability and a visionary outlook. As we set the stage for our own financial triumphs, let us draw from the lessons of global business leaders like Branson, understanding that strategic decision-making, resilience, and a clear vision are fundamental elements in the pursuit of enduring financial success.

THE PSYCHOLOGY OF MONEY

The psychology of money is a fascinating exploration into the intricate ways in which our thoughts, emotions, and behaviors shape our financial decisions. It delves into the psychological underpinnings that influence how we earn, spend, save, and invest. One of the most illuminating works on this subject comes from the acclaimed author Daniel Kahneman in his book "Thinking, Fast and Slow."

Kahneman, a Nobel laureate in Economics, delves into the complexities of human decision-making, shedding light on the cognitive biases and heuristics that impact our financial choices. In his exploration, Kahneman distinguishes between two systems of thinking: the fast, intuitive, and emotional "System 1" and the slow, deliberate, and logical "System 2." Understanding these systems provides insights into the psychology of money, revealing why individuals often deviate from rational financial behavior.

The psychological aspects of money are deeply rooted in our emotions, experiences, and societal influences. Behavioral economics, as explored by Kahneman, helps us comprehend why individuals may succumb to cognitive biases such as loss aversion, overconfidence, or the endowment effect. These biases can lead to suboptimal financial decisions, impacting our ability to save, invest wisely, and plan for the future.

Recognizing the psychological dimensions of money is crucial for making informed financial decisions. It involves understanding how emotions like fear, greed, and anxiety can shape our choices. Moreover, it prompts us to reflect on the influence of societal norms and peer pressure on our spending patterns.

As we navigate the psychology of money, it's essential to cultivate financial self-awareness. This self-awareness empowers us to recognize our biases, challenge ingrained beliefs, and make more deliberate financial choices. By incorporating the insights from Kahneman's "Thinking, Fast and Slow," we gain a deeper understanding of the intricate interplay between our cognitive processes and financial behavior.

In the exploration of the psychology of money, we embark on a journey of self-discovery and empowerment. Armed with knowledge, we can navigate the complexities of our financial minds, making decisions that align with our long-term goals and aspirations. As we delve into the psychology of money, let us heed the wisdom of Daniel Kahneman, acknowledging the profound impact our thought processes have on the intricate dance between ourselves and our finances.

CHAPTER 1

THE FOUNDATION OF WEALTH

The foundation of wealth is intricately tied to the first and fundamental step: savings. Saving is the cornerstone upon which financial security is built, representing the initial stride on the path to prosperity. It's the conscious decision to set aside a portion of one's income, creating a reservoir of resources that forms the bedrock for future financial endeavors.

As the starting step to wealth, savings serve a dual purpose. Firstly, it provides a safety net, offering a buffer against unforeseen expenses and economic uncertainties. This financial cushion shields individuals from the impact of unexpected challenges, fostering stability and peace of mind.

Secondly, savings form the basis for investment—the engine that propels wealth creation. By consistently setting aside a portion of income, individuals accumulate capital that can be strategically deployed in various investment avenues. This, in turn, leverages the power of compounding, a force that multiplies wealth over time.

Warren Buffett's wisdom resonates profoundly in the context of this foundational step: "Do not save what is left after spending, but spend what is left after saving." This succinct advice encapsulates the essence of prioritizing savings as a proactive and intentional act.

It emphasizes that wealth creation begins with a commitment to saving first, instilling the discipline needed to allocate resources wisely.

The starting step of savings, when approached with discipline and a long-term perspective, lays a sturdy foundation for the broader journey toward financial success. It is a foundational principle that transcends income levels and financial expertise, making the pursuit of wealth accessible to all who recognize the transformative potential of this essential first step.

Understanding the Importance of Saving

Little drops of water make a mighty ocean." This timeless proverb encapsulates the essence of the importance of savings in building wealth. Just as each drop contributes to the vastness of the ocean, every small amount saved contributes to the creation of substantial financial reserves over time. This simple yet profound quote serves as a reminder that consistent and disciplined savings, no matter how modest, have the potential to accumulate and create a significant impact on one's financial well-being. Just as the ocean is formed by the aggregation of countless droplets, so too is financial success crafted by the accumulation of incremental savings.

Understanding the importance of savings is akin to appreciating the power of delayed gratification and the potential for financial security. Let's delve into this concept through a practical example that illustrates the transformative impact of disciplined savings.

Consider two individuals, Alex and Taylor, both starting their careers at the age of 25. Alex adopts a proactive approach to personal finance, diligently setting aside a percentage of their income for savings, while Taylor, although earning a similar income, opts for a more laissez-faire attitude toward spending and saving.

Over the years, Alex consistently saves a portion of their income, diligently contributing to a retirement account and building an emergency fund. On the other hand, Taylor, while enjoying the present, often finds themselves strapped for cash and relying on credit when unexpected expenses arise.

Fast forward a decade, and both Alex and Taylor face a turning point. Alex's disciplined savings have not only provided financial security during emergencies but have also accumulated interest and returns through strategic investments. This financial growth has positioned Alex to make substantial investments, perhaps in real estate or starting a business, paving the way for diversified income streams.

On the contrary, Taylor, having lived without a structured savings plan, now grapples with mounting debt and missed opportunities. The absence of a financial safety net means that Taylor faces greater stress during unexpected financial challenges and misses out on the compounding growth that Alex has experienced.

This practical example underscores the importance of savings as a cornerstone of financial success. Alex's deliberate savings have not only cushioned against unforeseen events but have also laid the groundwork for broader financial endeavors. The example illustrates that savings extend beyond mere accumulation; they are a dynamic force that empowers individuals to navigate life's uncertainties while capitalizing on opportunities for growth.

In essence, understanding the importance of savings involves recognizing that it is not solely about forgoing present pleasures but rather a strategic investment in one's future. By adopting a disciplined savings approach, individuals, like Alex, can transform their financial landscapes, embracing a future of security, growth, and the realization of long-term aspirations.

Building a Solid Financial Foundation

Imagine your finances as a flourishing garden, where the act of saving becomes the essential nutrient enriching the soil. The first step in establishing a resilient financial foundation involves strategically planting the seeds of mindful budgeting. Similar to how a gardener allocates resources, budgeting channels your income, with a deliberate focus on nurturing the habit of saving.

Saving, in this analogy, is not just a task but the very essence that fosters growth. It's the water that quenches the thirst of your financial aspirations, allowing your financial garden to thrive. Just as a gardener meticulously tends to the growth of plants, consistent saving cultivates a robust core for your financial well-being.

Picture your emergency fund as the protective layer of soil encircling your financial garden. Life's unpredictable storms can strike, but with a well-nourished emergency fund, you have a buffer, ensuring that your financial garden remains resilient in the face of unexpected challenges.

Debt, in the context of this metaphor, is akin to invasive weeds that threaten to strangle your garden. Tending to your financial landscape involves weeding out these debts, clearing the ground for healthier financial growth.

Insurance, much like a gardener's watchful eye, shields your financial garden from potential pests and diseases. It provides a protective layer, ensuring that unforeseen circumstances don't devastate the fruits of your labor.

Investments become the diverse array of plants strategically placed to bring vibrancy and growth to your financial garden. By wisely choosing where to invest, you ensure a bountiful harvest in the future.

Continuous learning, akin to a gardener's exploration of new techniques and plant varieties, keeps your financial landscape vibrant. Staying informed about financial trends and strategies allows you to adapt your gardening practices, ensuring that your financial garden remains evergreen.

In the cultivation of your financial garden, saving becomes the lifeblood, fostering intentional growth and ensuring that your financial landscape flourishes through every season of life.

Breaking Free from the Cycle of Living from Paycheck to Paycheck

I consider this one of the most important sections of this book as 98% of the world live on their paychecks either as individuals or as a family.

Escaping the repetitive cycle of living paycheck to paycheck is a transformative journey that hinges on a single, powerful key—savings. Imagine savings as the catalyst for breaking free from the financial treadmill, unlocking a path toward stability and freedom.

In the monotonous rhythm of paycheck-to-paycheck living, the perpetual struggle to meet immediate needs often overshadows the potential for long-term financial empowerment. However, by redefining the role of savings, a significant shift occurs. It starts with viewing every dollar not just as a tool for momentary relief but as a strategic instrument for building a secure future.

Crafting a budget emerges as a compass, guiding this shift toward financial independence. The focus shifts from restriction to liberation—channeling income purposefully, discerning between needs and wants, and making intentional choices that align with overarching financial objectives. With savings taking center stage, the shackles of living paycheck to paycheck gradually give way.

Emergency savings, fueled by consistent contributions, becomes the safety net that prevents a relapse into the cycle when unexpected financial challenges arise. It signifies the realization that financial security is not an elusive dream but a tangible goal within reach.

As debts are strategically addressed and reduced, the burden of financial strain begins to lift. Savings, acting as both a catalyst for debt reduction and a source of financial resilience, becomes the linchpin in dismantling the cycle of perpetual financial stress.

Investing, traditionally considered beyond the reach of those navigating paycheck-to-paycheck living, becomes an attainable avenue for wealth-building. Savings, now redirected toward investments, transforms into a force that propels individuals toward a future characterized by financial autonomy.

In this narrative of liberation, savings emerges as the primary protagonist—a beacon of financial empowerment. Breaking free from the paycheck-to-paycheck cycle becomes a story of embracing the transformative potential of savings, one dollar at a time, and paving the way toward a life unburdened by the limitations of financial insecurity.

CHAPTER 2

BUDGETING BASICS

Budgeting is the cornerstone of financial well-being, offering a roadmap to navigate income and expenses strategically. At its core, budgeting is not about restriction but empowerment—providing a clear framework to achieve financial goals. One crucial reason to embrace budgeting is to prioritize savings.

Creating a budget involves assessing income and allocating resources thoughtfully. By incorporating savings as a non-negotiable item in the budget, individuals ensure that a portion of their earnings is systematically set aside for future needs and goals. This intentional act transforms budgeting from a mere accounting exercise to a tool for wealth-building.

Savings, embedded within the budget, serves as a financial safety net. It allows for the creation of emergency funds, shielding individuals from unexpected expenses and providing a sense of security. In the event of unforeseen challenges, having savings as an integral part of the budget provides a buffer, preventing financial stress and the need to dip into debt.

Moreover, budgeting cultivates a mindful spending habit. By categorizing expenses and aligning them with priorities, individuals become more conscious of where their money goes. This heightened awareness facilitates better decision-making, enabling individuals to cut unnecessary expenditures and redirect those funds toward savings, thereby fueling financial growth.

In essence, budgeting basics are not just about tracking expenses; they are a strategic tool to optimize financial health. By embracing budgeting and making savings a fundamental element, individuals can build a resilient financial foundation, achieve goals, and pave the way for a future of financial security and prosperity.

The Art of Budgeting

The art of budgeting is a delicate dance that transforms the mundane task of managing finances into a strategic and empowering process. It is not just about numbers on a spreadsheet but a dynamic and creative approach to achieving financial goals. Here's a glimpse into the artistry of budgeting:

Imagine budgeting as a canvas awaiting your strokes, each line and color representing a financial choice and decision. The first stroke involves understanding your income—a broad sweep that establishes the foundation of your financial masterpiece. It's about recognizing the palette of resources at your disposal.

Next comes the intricate detail work—allocating funds to various categories like housing, utilities, groceries, and, most importantly, savings. The art of budgeting isn't just about where money goes but about consciously deciding where it should go. It's a meticulous process of shaping your financial landscape, creating a harmonious balance between spending and saving.

Savings, in this artistic creation, serves as the focal point—a vibrant hue that adds depth and richness to the canvas. The deliberate strokes of allocating a portion of your income to savings are akin to building layers of financial security. It's the artist's signature, signifying a commitment to a future of stability and prosperity.

As you navigate the curves and lines of discretionary spending, the art of budgeting encourages mindfulness. It's about making intentional choices, understanding the value of each stroke on the canvas of your financial life. This awareness transforms budgeting from a rigid exercise into a dynamic process, allowing for adaptability and refinement over time.

Budgeting, at its essence, is an expression of priorities. It's about deciding what matters most to you and allocating resources accordingly. The artistry lies in finding the balance between enjoying the present and investing in the future—creating a masterpiece that evolves as your financial journey unfolds.

In the symphony of income and expenses, the art of budgeting provides the conductor's baton. It allows you to orchestrate your financial resources in a way that resonates with your life's goals and aspirations. Through this artistic approach, budgeting transcends the mundane and becomes a tool for crafting a future that reflects your unique vision and financial well-being.

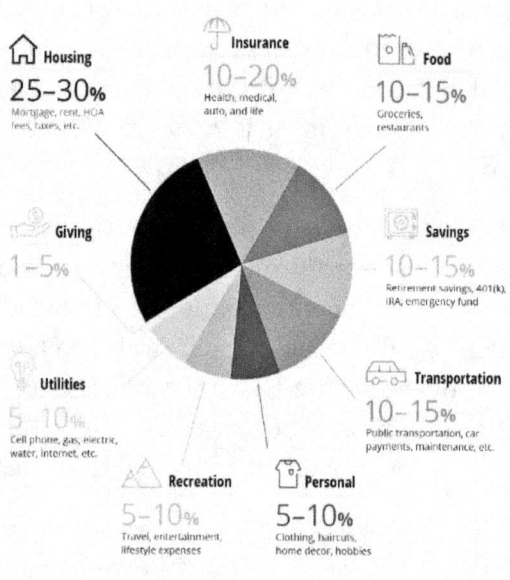

Ill 1.1

With Reference to the image above, one can also increase their savings by constraining some aspect of recreation, feeding expenses, giving, and personal expenses. This should increase your saving percentage and help you reach your savings goals faster.

Creating a Realistic Spending Plan

Crafting a realistic spending plan involves a thoughtful exploration of your financial landscape. Start by gaining a comprehensive understanding of your income sources, from salaries to freelance endeavors. This foundational step provides a clear picture of the financial canvas you'll be working with.

Next, categorize your expenses into fixed and variable costs. Fixed expenses, such as rent and utilities, are constants, while variable expenses, including entertainment and hobbies, offer flexibility. Distinguish between needs and wants, recognizing the non-negotiable essentials and the discretionary elements that can be adjusted based on available funds.

With this clarity, allocate specific amounts to each spending category, taking into account your income and priorities. This intentional distribution ensures a structured guide on how much can be spent in each area without exceeding your overall budget.

Consider the creation of an emergency fund as a pivotal element within your spending plan. Allocate a portion of your income to savings, catering to both short-term and long-term financial goals. This financial cushion becomes essential for unexpected expenses, contributing to your overall financial stability.

If you carry debts, allocate a portion of your budget to debt repayment. Prioritize high-interest debts while ensuring minimum payments on all obligations. This strategic approach enables gradual debt reduction without compromising your financial health.

Regularly monitor your spending plan and track actual expenditures. This ongoing assessment allows you to identify any deviations and make necessary adjustments. Flexibility is key; be willing to refine your plan based on changing circumstances or unforeseen expenses.

Ensure that your spending plan is sustainable over the long term. Be realistic about your financial situation and lifestyle. Striking a balance between adherence to financial goals and comfort in your daily life is crucial for the longevity and effectiveness of your spending plan.

Should you encounter challenges or uncertainties, consider seeking advice from financial professionals. Their insights can provide strategies to navigate specific financial hurdles and refine your spending plan for optimal financial health.

In essence, creating a realistic spending plan is a nuanced exploration of your financial journey. It's a personalized, dynamic process that serves as a tool for informed decision-making, aligning with your goals and accommodating your unique lifestyle.

Identify & Eliminate Financial Risks

Securing your financial future involves a nuanced approach to identifying and eliminating potential risks. Start by comprehensively assessing your financial landscape. Identify both external factors, like market fluctuations or job instability, and internal factors influenced by your financial decisions.

Establishing emergency funds is a fundamental step in building financial resilience. These funds act as a safety net, providing a cushion against unexpected expenses such as medical emergencies or job loss. Aim to save three to six months' worth of living expenses to enhance your overall financial stability.

If you're engaged in investments, diversification is key. Spread your investments across various assets and industries to minimize the impact of a downturn in any specific sector. This strategic move helps mitigate risks associated with market fluctuations.

Insurance coverage is a powerful tool in managing financial risks. Ensure you have adequate health, life, and property insurance to protect against unforeseen circumstances. These policies act as safeguards, preventing significant financial setbacks in challenging times.

Prioritize paying down high-interest debt to reduce financial vulnerability. This strategic move minimizes interest payments and frees up resources for savings and investments, contributing to a more secure financial future.

Regularly conduct financial health checkups to reassess your goals, evaluate risk tolerance, and adjust your financial strategy accordingly. Stay informed about economic trends, investment strategies, and personal finance to make informed decisions and adapt to changing circumstances.

Addressing legal and estate planning considerations is crucial for managing financial risks. Establish wills, trusts, and powers of attorney to ensure that your financial affairs align with your wishes, reducing the risk of legal complications or financial disputes.

Develop contingency plans for potential disruptions, such as job loss or economic downturns. Having a clear strategy for navigating these challenges, such as a budget for reduced income, enhances your ability to adapt with resilience.

In essence, securing your financial future requires a multifaceted approach. By building emergency funds, diversifying investments, securing insurance coverage, and staying informed, you position yourself to weather unforeseen challenges and foster a stable financial foundation.

CHAPTER 3

THE MAGIC OF COMPOUND INTEREST

The magic of compound interest is a financial phenomenon that can work wonders for wealth creation, especially when linked to a disciplined approach to savings. Compound interest is not just a mathematical concept; it's a powerful force that amplifies the growth of your money over time.

When you save money, it earns interest. Compound interest takes this a step further by calculating interest not only on your initial savings but also on the accumulated interest from previous periods. In simple terms, you earn interest not just on your principal amount but also on the interest that has already been added to your savings. This compounding effect accelerates wealth accumulation. Over the long term, even modest savings can grow substantially, creating a snowball effect. The earlier you start saving, the more time your money has to compound, magnifying the overall impact on your wealth.

For example, imagine saving a certain amount consistently over the years. The initial savings generate interest, and as time goes on, the interest itself earns more interest. This compounding process leads to exponential growth, significantly boosting the value of your savings.

Linking compound interest with a consistent savings plan becomes a potent strategy for wealth creation. It emphasizes the importance of starting early and staying committed to regular savings. The compounding magic works best when given the gift of time.

In summary, the magic of compound interest underscores the transformative potential of savings over time. By harnessing the power of compounding through consistent and early savings, individuals can pave the way for substantial wealth creation and financial security in the long run.

Unveiling the Eighth Wonder of the World

Welcome, prestigious audience, to the spectacular unveiling of a phenomenon so remarkable that it ranks as the world's eighth wonder. However, nature did not carve this marvel or etch it in stone. Rather, it originates from the complex world of personal finance- a mysterious force called ***the magic of compound interest***. As we explore this extraordinary show that defies conventional wonders and shapes destinies through the alchemy of financial wisdom, get ready to be intrigued.

Picture this as a mesmerizing journey where the act of saving ceases to be a mere accumulation of funds; instead, it becomes a process of compounding growth that defies the limits of the expected. Consider a modest stream of savings, gracefully navigating the currents of compound interest, transforming into a stream of wealth. The essence of this wonder lies in its unique ability to amplify the impact of even the smallest contributions, creating a perpetual cycle of growth that gains momentum over time.

Certainly, let's delve deeper into the magic of compound interest with a more extensive exploration, accompanied by mathematical illustrations.

Imagine your savings as seeds planted in the fertile soil of financial growth. Compound interest, our eighth wonder, is the sunlight and rain that nurtures these seeds, transforming them into a flourishing forest of wealth. As we journey into the intricacies, let's explore how this phenomenon works mathematically.

The Formula:

The heart of compound interest lies in a simple yet powerful formula: $A = P (1 + r/n)^{nt}$, where:

- A is the future value of the investment/loan, including interest.

- P is the principal amount (initial investment).

- r is the annual interest rate (as a decimal).

- n is the number of times that interest is compounded per unit t.

- t is the time the money is invested or borrowed for, in years.

Illustration 1: Annual Compounding:

Let's consider an initial investment (P) of $1,000 at an annual interest rate (r) of 5%, compounded annually ($n = 1$), over a period of 5 years ($t = 5$).

$$A = 1000 \times (1 + 0.05/1)^{1 \times 5}$$

$$A = 1000 \times (1.05)^5$$

$$A \approx 1000 \times 1.27628$$

$$A \approx 1276.28$$

So, after 5 years, the investment grows to approximately $1,276.28.

Illustration 2: Quarterly Compounding:

Now, let's explore quarterly compounding ($n = 4$) over the same period.

$$A = 1000 \times (1 + 0.05/4)^{4 \times 5}$$

$$A = 1000 \times (1.0125)^{20}$$

$$A \approx 1000 \times 1.28008$$

$$A \approx 1280.08$$

Quarterly compounding yields slightly more: approximately $1,280.08.

Illustration 3: Time's Impact:

Let's emphasize the impact of time. If we extend the period to 10 years while keeping the other parameters constant, the growth becomes even more pronounced.

$$A = 1000 \times (1 + 0.05/1)^{1 \times 10}$$

$$A \approx 1000 \times (1.05)^{10}$$

$$A \approx 1000 \times 1.628$$

$$A \approx 1628$$

After 10 years, the investment reaches approximately $1,628.

Conclusion:

These mathematical illustrations demonstrate the exponential growth facilitated by compound interest. It's not just about the *interest on the initial investment*; it's about *interest earning interest*, creating a compounding effect that accelerates wealth accumulation over time. The eighth wonder, with its mathematical elegance, showcases the transformative power of disciplined savings and the magic embedded within the formula. As time becomes an ally, the numbers reveal a wealth-building journey that goes beyond expectations.

Harnessing the Power of Time in Investing

As our journey through the financial landscape deepens, we now turn our gaze toward an elemental force that shapes destinies and molds fortunes—the relentless passage of time. In the continuum of our exploration, time emerges as the silent architect of wealth, weaving its influence through the very fabric of investing.

Consider, if you will, the profound dance between time and the compounding effect. This symbiotic relationship is no less than a financial alchemy, where each tick of the clock transforms a modest investment into a thriving ecosystem of wealth. It is not merely about earning interest on the principal; it's the symphony of interest earning interest, an echo that reverberates through the corridors of time. In the embrace of time, returns are not just multiplied; they are amplified. The more patient the investor, the more substantial the potential for growth. This amplification is not a hurried crescendo but a gradual and steady rise, a testament to the enduring power of a strategic and long-term investment approach.

Market volatility, that tempestuous companion on the financial journey, becomes more manageable with the cloak of time. While the markets may sway in the short term, the long-term trajectory tends to be a northward ascent. Time acts as a buffer, allowing investors to navigate the peaks and valleys with a steady hand and unwavering resolve.

Dollar-cost averaging, a technique that blends seamlessly with the tapestry of time, unfolds as a disciplined art. Regular contribution, regardless of market conditions, become a rhythmic dance with the market's heartbeat. This dance, orchestrated by time, ensures that investors benefit from market fluctuations, buying more when prices are low and fewer when prices are high.

Yet, time is not just a mathematical variable in this equation; it is the unseen architect of emotional resilience. Investors with a longer time horizon cultivate a resilience that withstands the whims of the market. The ebb and flow of short-term fluctuations become mere ripples in the grander scheme of long-term wealth creation.

Beyond the financial realm, time becomes a key player in the theater of goal achievement. Whether it's the dream of retirement, homeownership, or securing a child's education, the longer the runway, the more attainable these dreams become. Time provides the space for strategic planning, adjusting the course as life unfolds, and aligning investments with the rhythm of personal aspirations.

In this continuation of our financial odyssey, time emerges not as a constraint but as a boundless ally. It is the secret ingredient that transforms the mundane act of investing into a journey of abundance. As we sail through the currents of time, the promise of compounding growth and amplified returns beckons— a promise that extends an invitation to each reader, encouraging them to navigate the river of time with patience, wisdom, and the foresight to cultivate a flourishing financial future.

Maximizing Returns through Compound Growth

Maximizing returns through compound growth is a financial strategy akin to planting seeds and watching a garden flourish over time. At its core is the principle of compound interest, a powerful force that transforms modest savings into substantial wealth. Let's explore this concept, drawing parallels to the organic growth observed in nature.

Imagine your savings as seeds planted in fertile soil. Compound interest acts as the sunlight and rain that nurtures these seeds, enabling them to sprout and multiply. As you consistently contribute to your savings, compound interest becomes the catalyst for exponential growth. The interest earned doesn't just accumulate on the initial investment; it also compounds on the interest previously earned, creating a compounding effect that accelerates over time.

Much like a well-tended garden, where each plant contributes to the overall ecosystem, your savings, coupled with compound interest, contribute to the flourishing financial landscape. The key lies in patience and consistency. The longer your savings remain invested, the more time compound interest has to work its magic, gradually transforming small contributions into a significant financial harvest.

Consider this: By harnessing compound growth, you not only earn interest on your principal but also on the interest earned in previous periods. It's a cycle of growth that snowballs over time. This compounding effect becomes particularly potent when applied to long-term savings goals, such as retirement planning or building a nest egg for a major life event.

Just as a gardener reaps the rewards of careful cultivation, a saver benefits from the discipline of consistent contributions and the patience to allow compound interest to work its magic. This strategy requires a commitment to regular savings, an understanding of the power of time, and a long-term perspective.

In the realm of finance, maximizing returns through compound growth is not a sprint but a marathon. It's about recognizing the compounding power of your savings and allowing time to be your ally. As your financial garden grows, so does the potential for achieving your long-term financial aspirations, making compound growth an essential element in the journey toward enduring financial prosperity.

CHAPTER 4

OVERCOMING SAVING MYTH & OBSTACLES

In this chapter, we confront prevalent myths and obstacles that hinder individuals from realizing the full potential of saving. By dispelling misconceptions, we aim to liberate readers from self-imposed limitations and set the stage for a more robust financial future.

One widely held myth addressed here is the belief that saving is exclusively for the affluent. We challenge this notion, emphasizing that saving is a universal principle accessible to individuals at every income level. The chapter underscores that even modest, consistent contributions can lead to significant financial growth over time.

This chapter also addresses obstacles to saving, including procrastination and lack of financial literacy. Practical strategies are provided to help readers overcome these challenges, empowering them to take proactive steps toward building a solid financial foundation.

In essence, this chapter serves as a guide to untangling the misconceptions surrounding saving, fostering a mindset shift, and clearing the path for readers to embrace the empowering journey of financial security and prosperity.

Dispelling Common Misconceptions

In this section, we hope to eliminate some common misconceptions that often cast a shadow on the transformative potential of saving. By unraveling some of these misconceptions, we aim to empower readers with a renewed understanding of the accessible and universal nature of building financial security.

Misconception 1: "Saving is only for the wealthy."

It's a widespread misconception that saving is a financial privilege exclusive to the wealthy. In reality, saving is a universal practice accessible to individuals across all income brackets. It transcends socioeconomic boundaries, and even small, consistent contributions can lay the groundwork for significant financial growth. By dispelling this myth, we empower individuals to recognize the transformative potential of saving regardless of their current financial standing.

Misconception 2: "Saving requires significant sacrifice."

The belief that saving demands a substantial sacrifice in one's quality of life often deters individuals from embracing this essential financial practice. However, the reality is quite the opposite. Saving is not about deprivation but about achieving balance and making intentional choices. It encourages thoughtful decision-making, ensuring that financial goals align harmoniously with both immediate needs and long-term aspirations. By challenging this misconception, we redefine the narrative around saving as a pathway to financial stability without compromising one's lifestyle.

Misconception 3: "I'll start saving when I have more money."

Procrastination, rooted in the belief that meaningful saving requires larger sums, is a common obstacle. Contrary to this misconception, the essence of saving lies in initiating the process with whatever amount is feasible today. While starting early is advantageous, the power of compounding can still be harnessed by commencing the saving journey now, irrespective of the starting point. This dispels the notion that one must wait for a more significant income to experience the benefits of saving.

Misconception 4: "I don't need to save; I have a stable income."

The assumption that a stable income eliminates the need for saving is a risky misconception. Financial stability is not synonymous with immunity to unforeseen challenges. Savings, especially in the form of an emergency fund, is a proactive strategy to navigate unexpected financial hurdles. This misconception underscores the universal importance of saving as a tool for financial resilience, irrespective of the perceived stability of one's income.

Misconception 5: "I'm too old to start saving now."

While the advantages of initiating a saving practice early in life are evident, the belief that it's too late to begin later in life is a limiting misconception. Understanding the dynamics of compound growth reveals that even in later years, initiating a consistent saving practice can yield meaningful results. By dispelling this misconception, we empower individuals of all ages to recognize the enduring benefits of intentional saving and take proactive steps toward securing their financial well-being.

Navigating Emotional Challenges in Savings

Embarking on the journey towards financial security is an intricate process, intertwining practical steps with the complex landscape of our emotions and attitudes towards money. This delicate dance necessitates a nuanced approach, where self-awareness, discipline, and compassion converge to navigate the emotional challenges inherent in savings.

Many individuals grapple with the fear of the unknown or the anxiety induced by unexpected expenses, both of which can significantly impede consistent savings. Recognizing these fears and breaking down overarching financial goals into smaller, more manageable steps is an initial stride toward cultivating financial resilience. Establishing an emergency fund further acts as a safety net, providing a buffer against unforeseen financial setbacks and alleviating the anxiety stemming from the uncertainty of the future.

Impulse spending, a common challenge, often undermines dedicated efforts to save. Implementing a deliberate cooling-off period for non-essential purchases and identifying triggers for impulsive spending constitute effective strategies. By fostering a mindful approach to financial choices, individuals can redirect their resources towards savings rather than succumbing to the allure of momentary indulgences.

Envy and comparison can cast shadows on the savings journey, inducing feelings of inadequacy or impatience. Shifting the focus from external benchmarks to personal financial goals becomes imperative. Celebrating small victories and acknowledging the uniqueness of each individual's financial trajectory helps dismantle the comparison trap, fostering a more positive and realistic perspective on one's own financial path.

Guilt and regret, often associated with past financial mistakes, pose additional emotional hurdles in the pursuit of savings. The pathway to overcoming these challenges involves a transformative perspective shift – forgiving oneself for past missteps and viewing them as invaluable learning opportunities. Channeling any residual guilt into positive action, such as committing to better financial habits, empowers individuals to break free from the shackles of past financial misjudgments.

Procrastination, rooted in the fear of making incorrect financial decisions, can impede progress. To counter this tendency, breaking down overarching savings goals into smaller, more achievable tasks is essential. Creating a structured timeline and implementing a reward system can transform the process into a series of manageable steps, making the journey towards financial security less daunting.

The desire for immediate results is another emotional challenge that many individuals face. Impatience with the progress of savings can lead to frustration. Cultivating patience involves a focus on the long-term benefits of saving, understanding that progress may not always be linear, and regularly reviewing and adjusting financial goals to align with evolving circumstances.

Dealing with unexpected life changes, such as job loss or health issues, is a reality that can derail even the most robust savings plans. Building a resilient emergency fund becomes paramount in such situations. Additionally, adapting financial goals and contributions during challenging times, coupled with seeking support when needed, helps individuals navigate these unexpected twists in life's journey without sacrificing long-term financial stability.

Understanding and addressing these emotional challenges in savings is a crucial aspect of achieving enduring financial well-being. By navigating these emotions with empathy, resilience, and a strategic mindset, individuals can cultivate a healthier relationship with money, transforming the savings journey into a more sustainable and fulfilling pursuit.

Strategies for Consistent and Sustainable savings

Embarking on the journey of consistent and sustainable savings requires breaking down overwhelming financial goals into smaller, more manageable steps. This phased approach facilitates a sense of accomplishment and mitigates anxiety.

First, we must learn to combat impulse spending by use of deliberate measures. Implementing a cooling-off period for non-essential expenses enables thoughtful decision-making. Understanding and addressing the emotional triggers behind impulsive spending allows individuals to redirect resources towards savings, fostering a more mindful approach to financial choices.

Cultivating patience in savings involves focusing on the long-term benefits. Regularly reviewing and adjusting financial goals to align with evolving circumstances is crucial. Recognizing that progress in savings, much like other aspects of life, may not always follow a linear trajectory is essential.

Counteracting procrastination in savings requires breaking down overarching goals into smaller, more achievable tasks. Establishing a structured timeline with milestones and implementing a reward system transforms the savings process into a series of manageable steps, turning procrastination into a proactive approach.

Embracing continuous learning and adaptability involves staying informed about financial trends and strategies. Being adaptable and ready to adjust savings plans in response to changing circumstances ensures that savings remain dynamic and responsive to the evolving financial environment.

In weaving these strategies into the fabric of one's financial journey, the emphasis is not solely on the practical aspects but also on the emotional and psychological elements. By integrating these strategies, individuals can navigate the complexities of consistent and sustainable savings with resilience, fostering a financial journey that is both enduring and fulfilling.

CHAPTER 5

THE MINDSET OF FINANCIAL SUCCESS

The mindset of financial success is rooted in a combination of discipline, adaptability, and a long-term perspective. It involves cultivating a habit of setting clear, achievable financial goals and consistently working towards them. A successful financial mindset embraces continuous learning about personal finance, allowing individuals to make informed decisions and adapt to changing economic landscapes. It involves understanding the value of patience, recognizing that wealth accumulation is often a gradual process. This mindset also encourages the development of a healthy relationship with money, emphasizing the importance of savings, investments, and mindful spending. Ultimately, a mindset geared towards financial success seeks to empower individuals to take control of their financial destinies, fostering resilience and a sense of accomplishment along the journey to financial well-being.

Cultivating a Wealth-Building Mindset

Cultivating a wealth-building mindset within the realm of saving requires a fundamental shift in perception. It's about viewing saving not as a restriction but as a conscious choice towards financial empowerment and security. Recognizing that each contribution to savings brings you closer to your financial aspirations is a crucial mindset shift.

Embrace the power of automation in your savings journey. Setting up automatic transfers to your savings account transforms saving from a conscious effort into a habitual practice, making it an integral part of your financial routine.

Prioritize the creation and maintenance of an emergency fund. Understand that this fund serves as more than just a safety net; it's a cornerstone for financial resilience, shielding you from unexpected expenses and allowing your wealth to grow uninterrupted.

Approach saving with the mindset of incremental increases. As your income grows or expenses decrease, channel those positive changes into higher savings contributions. This methodical approach ensures that saving becomes a dynamic and evolving aspect of your financial plan.

Connect your saving to specific financial goals, whether it's buying a home, starting a business, or funding your children's education. Having purposeful savings goals gives your financial journey direction and motivation.

Extend your understanding of savings beyond traditional accounts. Educate yourself on various investment opportunities aligned with your risk tolerance and financial goals. Recognizing the potential for growth beyond basic savings encourages a more proactive approach.

Periodically review and adjust your saving strategy, recognizing the importance of staying adaptable. Assess changes in your income, expenses, and financial goals, making adjustments to your savings plan accordingly.

Celebrate your savings milestones. Whether it's reaching a specific dollar amount or achieving a certain percentage of your financial goal, acknowledging these milestones reinforces the positive aspects of saving, motivating you to stay committed to your wealth-building journey.

Align your saving mindset with mindful spending. Evaluate your expenses and identify areas where adjustments can be made to redirect funds towards savings. It's about finding a balance that allows you to enjoy the present while securing your financial future.

Develop a sense of gratitude for your financial growth. Recognize and appreciate the progress you've made in your saving journey. This positive reinforcement strengthens your wealth-building mindset, creating a harmonious relationship with your financial well-being.

Aligning Financial Goals with Personal Values

Aligning financial goals with personal values is a strategic and empowering approach to wealth management. It involves not only setting tangible objectives but also ensuring that these objectives resonate with your core beliefs and aspirations.

Understanding your values lays the foundation for aligning financial goals. Take time to reflect on what truly matters to you—whether it's family, education, community, or personal growth. These values serve as guiding principles that shape your financial decisions.

Your financial goals should reflect your values and priorities. If family is a core value, your goals might include saving for a home to provide a stable environment. If education is crucial, financial aspirations should target funding academic pursuits.

Consider the long-term impact of your financial decisions on your values. How will your goals contribute to your well-being and the well-being of those you care about? Aligning financial goals with personal values ensures that your wealth-building journey is purposeful and fulfilling.

Be mindful of lifestyle choices and spending habits. Aligning financial goals with personal values often requires evaluating whether your current lifestyle aligns with your core beliefs. Adjustments may be necessary to direct resources toward goals that truly matter.

Regularly reassess your goals and values. As life evolves, so do values and priorities. Regularly reviewing and adjusting financial goals ensures they remain in harmony with your changing aspirations and circumstances. Celebrate milestones that align with your values. Acknowledge and celebrate achievements that reflect progress toward your financial goals and uphold your values. This positive reinforcement strengthens your commitment to the aligned financial journey.

Seek professional guidance to align strategies with values. Consulting financial advisors can help tailor investment strategies and financial plans that resonate with your values, ensuring a comprehensive alignment of your resources with your aspirations.

Embrace philanthropy as part of your financial journey. Aligning financial goals with personal values often includes giving back to causes that matter to you. Incorporating philanthropy into your wealth-building strategy fosters a sense of purpose and social impact.

Aligning financial goals with personal values is not just about accumulating wealth; it's about creating a financial narrative that aligns with your intrinsic beliefs and passions. This alignment not only contributes to a more fulfilling life but also reinforces the significance of your financial journey in the broader context of personal well-being.

Fostering a Healthy Relationship with Money

Fostering a healthy relationship with money involves cultivating a mindset that goes beyond mere transactions, emphasizing a balanced and purposeful approach to financial well-being.

Understanding the Emotional Aspect:

Recognize that money is not just a numerical value; it holds emotional weight. Acknowledge your feelings about money, whether it's anxiety, excitement, or stress, and work towards understanding and managing these emotions.

Mindful Spending Habits:

Develop mindful spending habits by aligning your purchases with your values and priorities. Consider the long-term impact of your spending choices on your financial goals, fostering a sense of purpose in your financial decisions.

Practicing Gratitude:

Cultivate a sense of gratitude for your current financial situation. Recognize the positive aspects of your financial journey, regardless of the scale, and appreciate the progress you've made. Gratitude contributes to a healthier mindset surrounding money.

Setting Realistic Goals:

Establish realistic and achievable financial goals that align with your aspirations. Whether it's building an emergency fund, paying off debt, or saving for a specific purpose, setting goals provides direction and motivation in your financial journey.

Learning and Growing:

Approach financial education as an ongoing journey. Continuously seek opportunities to enhance your financial literacy, understanding the nuances of investing, budgeting, and wealth-building. Embracing a growth mindset ensures adaptability in the ever-evolving financial landscape.

Balancing Lifestyle and Savings:

Strive for a balanced lifestyle that harmonizes enjoyment of the present with securing the future. Avoid extremes of overspending or excessive frugality, finding a middle ground that promotes financial stability while allowing for life's pleasures.

Open Communication:

Foster open communication about money within relationships. Discuss financial goals, expectations, and concerns with your partner, family, or close friends. Transparency reduces misunderstandings and promotes a collaborative approach to financial decision-making.

Embracing Financial Self-Care:

Treat your financial well-being with the same care as your physical and mental health. Implement self-care practices by regularly assessing and nurturing your financial situation. This may involve periodic financial check-ins, setting boundaries, and seeking professional advice when needed.

Building Resilience:

Understand that financial setbacks are a natural part of life. Building resilience involves adapting to challenges, learning from setbacks, and reframing them as opportunities for growth. A resilient mindset contributes to a healthier and more sustainable relationship with money.

CHAPTER 6

REAL LIFE STORIES OF FINANCIAL TRANSFORMATION

Experience they say is the best teacher but no one said you have to be the one experiencing the event or case. One can equally learn the lessons Mr. experience has to teach by listening to or reading other people's experience.

There is a wonderful quote from Sir Isaac Newton that goes, *"If I have seen further than others, it is by standing upon the shoulders of giants."*

As a result, this chapter will provide uninterrupted depth into practical case studies and stories of individuals who have gained experience in this journey of savings and wealth

Real Life Stories of Financial Transformation

1. The Debt-Free Journey of Sarah and Mike

Sarah and Mike, a young couple, embarked on a transformative journey to become debt-free. With a combined history of student loans, credit card debt, and car payments, they decided to take control of their financial destiny. By implementing a strict budget, aggressively paying down debts, and making intentional lifestyle changes, they not only eliminated their outstanding balances but also built an emergency fund and started investing. Their story serves as an inspiring example of how a deliberate focus on financial goals can lead to profound transformation.

2. From Financial Struggle to Entrepreneurial Success - The Story of Alex:

Alex went from financial struggle to entrepreneurial success. Faced with job instability and mounting bills, he decided to channel his passion into a side business. Through meticulous financial planning, he saved a portion of his income, which eventually became the seed capital for his venture. Despite initial challenges, his business flourished, and he not only achieved financial stability but also built wealth. Alex's story illustrates the power of combining passion with financial discipline for a remarkable transformation.

3. A Retirement Renaissance - The Journey of Emily:

Emily, approaching retirement age, discovered the need for a financial renaissance in her life. Realizing her retirement savings were insufficient, she decided to take proactive steps. Emily diligently researched investment options, adjusted her spending habits, and sought advice from financial professionals. Over time, her disciplined approach and strategic adjustments resulted in a significant increase in her retirement nest egg. Emily's story highlights that it's never too late to embark on a financial transformation with the right mindset and actions.

4. The Savvy Saver - James' Wealth Accumulation:

James, a meticulous saver and investor, exemplifies the impact of consistent saving and wise investments. Starting with modest savings early in his career, James maintained a disciplined approach, regularly increasing his contributions and diversifying his investments. Through the power of compounding and a patient long-term perspective, James accumulated substantial wealth over the years. His story emphasizes the importance of starting early, being consistent, and making informed financial decisions for long-term success.

5. Rising from Financial Adversity - Maria

Maria faced significant financial adversity, including job loss and unexpected medical expenses. She decided to rebuild her financial foundation. Maria embraced a frugal lifestyle, focused on building an emergency fund, and sought new income streams. Over time, she not only recovered from financial setbacks but also transformed her adversity into an opportunity to create a more resilient and secure financial future. Maria's story demonstrates the resilience that can emerge from financial challenges with determination and strategic planning.

These real-life case studies showcase diverse journeys of financial transformation, emphasizing the unique challenges individuals faced and the specific strategies they employed to achieve remarkable success in their financial lives.

Learning from the Journeys of Financial Success

Examining the financial success story of Warren Buffett, one of the world's most renowned businessmen and investors, provides valuable lessons for those seeking financial prosperity.

Warren Buffett's journey underscores the significance of adopting a long-term perspective in financial success. His renowned buy-and-hold strategy involves investing in fundamentally strong companies and holding onto them for extended periods, teaching the power of patience and the rewards of allowing investments to grow over time.

Buffett is a staunch advocate of value investing, emphasizing the importance of thoroughly understanding a company's intrinsic value before investing. This principle teaches us to approach investments with a focus on quality and a keen awareness of the underlying value, aligning with the core philosophy of making informed decisions.

Despite his immense success, Buffett maintains a relentless commitment to continuous learning. His voracious reading habits and dedication to staying informed about market trends highlight the importance of ongoing education in the world of finance, serving as a reminder that the pursuit of knowledge is a lifelong journey.

Buffett's approach to risk management is grounded in a deep understanding of the businesses he invests in. By investing in companies with strong fundamentals and competitive advantages, he mitigates risks associated with market volatility. This teaches us the importance of thorough research and risk assessment in financial decision-making.

Despite his vast wealth, Buffett maintains a famously frugal lifestyle, showcasing the importance of disciplined spending and avoiding unnecessary financial indulgences. This principle encourages individuals to prioritize saving and investing over extravagant consumption.

Buffett's success is also attributed to diversification and adaptability. While he has core investment principles, he's not afraid to adapt to changing market conditions. This flexibility and willingness to diversify his portfolio showcase the importance of being adaptable and open to new opportunities.

Buffett's commitment to philanthropy is evident through initiatives like the Giving Pledge. His dedication to giving back to society reinforces the idea that financial success should extend beyond personal gain, encouraging individuals to consider the broader impact of their wealth on the community.

Buffett emphasizes the importance of surrounding oneself with a competent and trustworthy team. His partnership with Charlie Munger and the team at Berkshire Hathaway exemplifies the value of collaboration and leveraging collective expertise in achieving financial success.

Buffett's resilience during market downturns, such as the 2008 financial crisis, teaches us the importance of maintaining composure and even seizing opportunities during challenging times. This resilience underscores the idea that market fluctuations are part of the investment journey, and staying the course can lead to long-term success.

In learning from Warren Buffett's financial success journey, individuals can glean insights into the importance of a long-term perspective, value-based decision-making, continuous learning, risk management, conservative financial habits, diversification, philanthropy, teamwork, and resilience. These principles offer a roadmap for those aspiring to achieve financial prosperity and make a positive impact in the world of finance.

Turning Adversity into Financial Triumph

Turning adversity into financial triumph is a testament to resilience, strategic thinking, and unwavering commitment to financial well-being. Individuals facing job loss often channel their skills into successful entrepreneurial ventures, showcasing the transformative power of innovation and determination. Many triumphs over overwhelming debt through disciplined financial strategies, such as careful budgeting and negotiation with creditors. Their stories highlight the transformative power of perseverance and financial planning in climbing out of debt.

Health challenges can strain finances, but stories of financial resilience emerge through proactive management of healthcare costs, securing insurance, and building emergency funds. These triumphs underscore the importance of preparing for unexpected financial challenges.

Navigating real estate market downturns strategically has proven to be a pathway to financial triumph. Investors who patiently wait for property values to rebound and make informed decisions on purchases often emerge with significant financial gains.

Individuals who faced financial setbacks, such as bankruptcy or business failures, have successfully rebuilt their financial lives. Learning from past mistakes, seeking professional advice, and implementing sound financial practices contribute to their recovery and greater financial success.

Educational and career pivots become avenues for financial triumph as individuals pursue new skills, retrain, or shift to industries with better prospects. This adaptability and commitment to continuous improvement led to enhanced earning potential and financial success.

Savvy investors turn economic downturns into opportunities by strategically adjusting their investment portfolios. Identifying undervalued assets, diversifying investments, and staying committed to a long-term vision enable them to capitalize on market recoveries and achieve substantial financial gains.

In these stories, the common thread is the ability to view adversity as an opportunity for growth, learning, and strategic decision-making. Whether through entrepreneurship, debt management, health challenges, real estate, financial setbacks, educational pivots, or investment strategies, individuals demonstrate that resilience and strategic thinking can lead to financial triumph in the face of adversity. Their stories inspire others to navigate challenges with a proactive mindset and transform adversity into a pathway to financial success.

CHAPTER 7

INVESTING IN YOUR FUTURE

Beyond Saving: The Role of Investing

Beyond saving, the role of investing plays a pivotal role in achieving long-term financial success. Saving provides a foundation, but investing allows for the growth of wealth over time. By strategically allocating funds to various investment vehicles, individuals have the potential to generate returns that outpace inflation and increase their overall financial net worth.

Investing offers the opportunity to build a diversified portfolio, spreading risk across different assets and optimizing potential returns. Whether through stocks, bonds, real estate, or other investment instruments, a well-balanced portfolio can provide a hedge against market fluctuations and contribute to sustained financial growth.

Moreover, investing is a means to harness the power of compounding, where earnings generate additional earnings over time. This compounding effect accelerates wealth accumulation, emphasizing the importance of an early start in the investment journey.

While saving ensures financial security, investing goes a step further by fostering the potential for wealth appreciation. It allows individuals to participate in the broader economic growth and capitalize on opportunities that may not be accessible through traditional savings alone.

In conclusion, the role of investing extends beyond mere saving, offering a dynamic pathway to financial prosperity. By understanding investment principles, diversifying portfolios, and embracing a long-term perspective, individuals can leverage the power of investing to enhance their financial well-being and secure a more robust financial future.

Diversifying Your Investment Portfolio

Diversifying your investment portfolio is a fundamental strategy that involves spreading your investments across different asset classes, industries, and geographic regions to manage risk and enhance potential returns. By allocating your funds to a variety of investments, you aim to create a more balanced and resilient portfolio.

A diversified investment approach mitigates the impact of poor performance in any single investment, as losses in one area may be offset by gains in others. This strategy is grounded in the principle of not putting all your eggs in one basket, acknowledging that different investments respond differently to market conditions.

One way to achieve diversification is by allocating your funds across various asset classes, such as stocks, bonds, and real estate. Each asset class has its own risk and return characteristics, and their performance may not be correlated. When one asset class underperforms, others may provide stability or growth, reducing the overall risk of your portfolio.

Within each asset class, further diversification can be achieved by selecting different securities. For instance, within the stock market, you can diversify by investing in a mix of large-cap and small-cap stocks, as well as across different industries. In bonds, diversification may involve varying maturities and credit qualities.

Geographic diversification is another key element. Investing in assets from different regions or countries can provide exposure to various economic conditions and reduce the impact of regional downturns on your portfolio.

While diversification doesn't guarantee profits or eliminate risk, it is a powerful risk management tool. It helps protect your investments from the volatility of specific sectors or markets, fostering a more stable and resilient portfolio.

Investors should regularly review and rebalance their portfolios to ensure that diversification remains effective. Market conditions and economic factors evolve, impacting the performance of different assets. Adjusting your portfolio to maintain a diversified allocation aligns with the dynamic nature of the financial markets.

In summary, diversifying your investment portfolio is a strategic approach to managing risk and enhancing potential returns. By spreading your investments across various assets, industries, and regions, you aim to create a well-balanced and resilient portfolio that can weather the fluctuations of the financial markets.

Having multiple streams of income in various sectors and different industries is also great as this tend to share the risk by allowing the success of the rest to cushion the damage or risk posed by one.

Balancing Risk and Reward

Balancing risk and reward are a delicate art in the realm of financial decision-making. It involves carefully weighing the potential benefits against the associated risks to achieve a harmonious equilibrium.

In navigating the financial landscape, individuals must consider the inherent risks that come with investment opportunities. Whether in the stock market, real estate, or entrepreneurial ventures, the potential for reward often correlates with a certain level of risk.

Understanding and managing this delicate balance is crucial for making informed financial choices.

Prudent risk management entails a thorough assessment of potential downsides and an awareness of one's risk tolerance. It involves aligning financial goals with an acceptable level of risk, acknowledging that different investments carry varying degrees of uncertainty. This approach ensures that individuals are neither overly cautious, missing out on growth opportunities, nor recklessly exposing themselves to undue financial peril.

The concept of risk and reward extends beyond investment decisions and permeates various aspects of financial planning. Balancing the pursuit of higher returns with the need for financial security, individuals often grapple with choices that involve short-term gains versus long-term stability. This balance requires a strategic approach that considers individual circumstances, time horizons, and overarching financial objectives.

In entrepreneurial endeavors, embracing risk is often an inherent part of innovation and growth. However, successful entrepreneurs understand the importance of calculated risk-taking. They meticulously analyze potential rewards, mitigate risks where possible, and make informed decisions that align with their business goals.

Balancing risk and reward are not a one-size-fits-all endeavor. It demands a personalized approach that considers individual financial circumstances, preferences, and aspirations. It requires continuous assessment and adaptation as financial landscapes evolve, markets fluctuate, and personal circumstances change.

Ultimately, achieving a balance between risk and reward is about making conscious and well-informed choices that align with one's financial goals. It's a dynamic process that involves staying informed, reassessing risk tolerances, and adjusting strategies as needed. Striking this delicate equilibrium empowers individuals to navigate the financial terrain with confidence, maximizing opportunities for growth while safeguarding against unnecessary risks.

CHAPTER 8

NAVIGATING ECONOMIC UNCERTAINTY

Building Resilience in Financial Planning

Building resilience in financial planning is crucial for navigating the uncertainties of life. Individuals who successfully incorporate resilience into their financial strategies often exhibit a capacity to adapt and overcome setbacks.

In facing unexpected expenses or income fluctuations, resilient financial planners maintain emergency funds. This provides a financial buffer, allowing them to address unforeseen challenges without derailing their long-term financial goals.

Furthermore, a resilient approach involves continuous learning about personal finance and investment strategies. This adaptability enables individuals to make informed decisions in response to evolving economic conditions, contributing to the overall resilience of their financial plans.

Embracing a mindset of flexibility is essential. Resilient financial planners understand that setbacks are a natural part of the financial journey. They view challenges not as roadblocks but as opportunities to learn, adjust, and strengthen their financial positions.

Collaboration with financial professionals is another aspect of building resilience. Seeking advice from experts helps individuals make well-informed decisions, particularly during complex financial situations or market uncertainties.

Ultimately, building resilience in financial planning involves a proactive approach, incorporating emergency funds, continuous learning, a flexible mindset, and collaboration with financial experts. This resilience equips individuals to navigate the dynamic landscape of personal finance, ensuring their long-term financial well-being.

Strategies for Thriving in Turbulent Times

Navigating turbulent times requires a strategic approach that blends resilience, adaptability, and sound financial principles. In the context of a book on saving and wealth, here are strategies for thriving in turbulent times:

1. Building a Robust Emergency Fund

Establishing and consistently contributing to an emergency fund is a fundamental strategy. Having a financial safety net provides peace of mind and safeguards against unexpected expenses, job loss, or economic downturns, ensuring you can weather financial storms without compromising long-term goals.

2. Diversification in Investments:

Embrace a diversified investment portfolio to mitigate risks associated with market fluctuations. A well-balanced mix of assets, such as stocks, bonds, and real estate, can help protect your wealth during economic uncertainties and capitalize on opportunities.

3. Strategic Debt Management:

Assess and manage debt strategically. In turbulent times, reducing high-interest debt and avoiding unnecessary loans can provide greater financial flexibility. Prioritize paying down debts strategically, focusing on those with higher interest rates.

4. Continuous Learning and Financial Literacy:

In ever-changing economic landscapes, continuous learning and financial literacy are powerful tools. Stay informed about economic trends, investment strategies, and personal finance principles. This knowledge equips you to make informed decisions and adapt your financial strategies accordingly.

5. Adaptive Budgeting:

Develop an adaptive budget that allows for flexibility in income and expenses. Consider potential fluctuations in income during turbulent times and adjust your budget accordingly. This proactive approach ensures financial stability and prevents the accumulation of unnecessary debt.

6. Resilient Mindset and Long-Term Focus:

Cultivate a resilient mindset that enables you to face challenges with a positive outlook. Maintain a long-term focus on your financial goals, understanding that short-term disruptions are part of the broader journey. A resilient mindset helps you persevere and make sound financial decisions despite uncertainties.

7. Maximizing Savings Opportunities:

Identify opportunities to maximize savings, even in challenging times. This could involve negotiating better deals on expenses, optimizing tax strategies, or exploring additional income streams. Strategic savings contribute to financial stability and provide a buffer during economic volatility.

8. Strategic Career Planning:

Invest in your professional development and consider strategic career planning. Acquiring in-demand skills and maintaining a strong professional network can enhance your employability and income potential, reducing vulnerability during economic downturns.

9. Collaborative Financial Planning:

Engage in collaborative financial planning with trusted professionals. Seek advice from financial advisors, accountants, and legal experts to ensure your financial strategies are robust and aligned with your long-term goals. Professional guidance can provide valuable insights during turbulent times.

10. Mindful Consumer Habits:

Adopt mindful consumer habits by distinguishing between needs and wants. During turbulent times, prioritizing essential expenses and avoiding unnecessary purchases can contribute significantly to savings and financial stability.

Incorporating these strategies into your financial plan enhances your ability to thrive in turbulent times. The combination of prudent saving, strategic investments, continuous learning, and a resilient mindset forms a solid foundation for building and preserving wealth in an ever-changing economic landscape.

Adapting to Changing Financial Landscapes

Adapting to changing financial landscapes is a fundamental skill in navigating the dynamic world of finance. It involves staying attuned to shifts in economic conditions, market trends, and regulatory changes to make informed decisions and thrive in evolving financial environments.

In the face of uncertainties, individuals must develop a proactive approach, embracing flexibility to adjust strategies as needed. This adaptability extends to various aspects of financial management, including investments, budgeting, and overall financial planning.

The ability to adapt becomes particularly crucial during economic downturns or periods of market volatility. Rather than succumbing to panic, individuals with a strong adaptive mindset assess the situation, reevaluate their financial goals, and make necessary adjustments to weather the storm.

Adapting to changing financial landscapes also involves leveraging technological advancements. Embracing digital tools, online resources, and fintech solutions can enhance financial management efficiency, offering new opportunities for investment, savings, and budget optimization.

Continuous learning is a key component of adapting to financial changes. Staying informed about emerging trends, investment opportunities, and regulatory shifts ensures individuals remain equipped to make well-informed decisions in an ever-evolving financial landscape.

In essence, adapting to changing financial landscapes is a dynamic process that involves proactive decision-making, flexibility, continuous learning, and leveraging technological advancements. Those who master this skill are better positioned to not only survive but thrive in the face of financial uncertainties.

Conclusion

In concluding this transformative journey through the pages of "Saving Can Make You Rich," we find ourselves at the intersection of financial wisdom and the promise of a brighter, more empowered future. This book has been a guide, a companion, and a source of inspiration, weaving together the threads of saving, investing, and adapting to changing financial landscapes.

As we close this chapter, let us reflect on the overarching theme that saving is not merely a financial habit but a powerful catalyst for wealth creation and financial freedom. The stories shared, the principles discussed, and the practical insights provided all converge to underscore the fundamental truth that small, consistent savings have the potential to lead to substantial financial growth.

Throughout these pages, we have delved into the minds of financial titans, explored the real-life stories of resilience and success, and dissected the intricacies of financial principles. From understanding the psychology of money to dispelling common misconceptions about savings, each chapter has been a stepping stone towards financial enlightenment.

The journey of financial success is not a one-size-fits-all endeavor; it is a dynamic and personalized expedition. It requires a mindset shift, a commitment to disciplined saving, and the flexibility to adapt to the ever-changing financial landscapes. The book has served as a compass, providing guidance on setting goals, making informed decisions, and embracing the transformative power of financial freedom.

As we close this chapter, let us carry forward the lessons learned, the principles embraced, and the vision of a financially liberated future. Let the journey of saving and financial empowerment be a continuous exploration, marked by resilience, adaptability, and the unwavering belief that, indeed, saving can make you rich in more ways than one.

May the insights gained within these pages serve as a compass on your ongoing journey towards financial prosperity and may the pursuit of financial freedom be not just a destination but a fulfilling and purpose-driven way of life. The book concludes, but your financial journey, enriched by the wisdom shared, is only just beginning. Here's to a future marked by financial resilience, abundance, and the realization that your commitment to saving can truly make you rich.

About the Author

David Mark, the esteemed author of "Saving Can Make You Rich," brings an impressive 30 years of expertise to the world of personal finance. With a robust background in finance, David has earned a stellar reputation as a seasoned professional and a trusted authority in the field.

Armed with a wealth of knowledge and experience, David Mark holds degrees in finance and has dedicated three decades to various roles within the financial industry. His journey has included pivotal positions such as financial advising, investment management, and roles in banking. This extensive hands-on experience has equipped him with a profound understanding of the intricate dynamics of personal finance.

David Mark's commitment to demystifying financial concepts is not confined to the professional realm. His passion for financial literacy and empowerment has driven him to contribute significantly to the field. Whether through articles, workshops, or contributions to reputable financial publications, David has consistently sought to make financial knowledge accessible to a broad audience.

Recognized for his ability to translate complex financial principles into practical, actionable advice, David Mark is a thought leader who values clarity and real-world application in his writing. The insights shared in "Saving Can Make You Rich" reflect his dedication to providing readers with actionable strategies and a clear roadmap toward financial success.

David Mark's enduring commitment to ongoing learning and adaptability positions him as a reliable source of guidance in navigating the ever-evolving landscape of personal finance. Readers can trust that the wisdom imparted in this book is not only rooted in David's 30 years of experience but also reflects a genuine desire to empower individuals on their unique journeys to financial prosperity.

www.ingramcontent.com/pod-product-compliance
Lightning Source LLC
Chambersburg PA
CBHW071100290526
45795CB00004B/1587